FROM A CHILD'S PERSPECTIVE

FROM A CHILD'S PERSPECTIVE

Alcoholism

Lars P. Hersom

BALBOA.
PRESS
A DIVISION OF HAY HOUSE

ISBN: 978-1-4525-5319-1 (sc)
ISBN: 978-1-4525-5318-4 (e)

Balboa Press books may be ordered through booksellers or by contacting:

Balboa Press
A Division of Hay House
1663 Liberty Drive
Bloomington, IN 47403
www.balboapress.com
1-(877) 407-4847

Printed in the United States of America

Balboa Press rev. date: 6/14/2012

A LETTER FROM THE AUTHOR

My father lost his life to an addiction to alcohol combined with adult onset diabetes in February 1999. In going through his belongings in the house I grew up in, I found notes he had written from some kind of alcoholics' program that he had been forced to go to after being arrested for OWI (Operating a motor vehicle While under the Influence of alcohol).

It was the most emotional time of my life and an extremely difficult thing to go through. From my perspective, the condition of the home had deteriorated to a place where no one would ever want to live, and he had lost his desire to live and to participate in family activities and events.

After his death, I found notes Dad had written about his drinking; he was obviously following a format or direction that he had to follow in a class, but the words touched my heart in so many ways.

In the days, weeks, and months to follow, I was constantly asking myself if I could have or should have done something to attempt to save him. I contacted someone to discuss the possibility of having him taken to a place to try to "dry out" and have a chance at a better quality of life. I was immediately told that while I had the power to do this, they had never seen it work unless the person came to them voluntarily. In other words, the person has to want to change on his own. I have found some peace in this, but still wonder if I could have done something to attempt to save him or help him improve his life and reel him back in to be closer to us.

DEDICATION

Respectfully written in loving memory of my father,
Wilbert "Bub" Amos Hersom

On the way to work on Friday, February 28, 2011, a thought come to my mind that literally gave me goose bumps: to reach out initially through a book about the experience of growing up in a home of an alcoholic. I also felt I could explain what it was like going through the life experiences, including the death of my father and the guilt and challenges that I faced. As I thought of this, I came to realize that the perspective was that of a child of an alcoholic. A book titled *From a Child's Perspective: Alcoholism* came to my mind.

This book's main objectives are to reach out to people, and hopefully, make a difference in someone's life so he or she may be able to avoid the ending that I experienced. I also hope to help the people who have these issues understand the impact they are having on the lives of the children and those who love them.

For me, no matter what age I reach, I will always be the child of an alcoholic and one whose children's lives were deprived of the relationship of a grandfather and one whose father's life was taken by an addiction to alcohol.

Lars P. Hersom

CONTENTS

CHAPTER 1 - WHO WAS HE?

"Hi, my name is Bub Hersom, and I'm an alcoholic." I can only imagine that this is the way the meetings for alcoholics started out. Sometimes I feel like I can almost sense the gut-wrenching, twisting feelings that I can only imagine he may have felt in saying these things or even the embarrassment and humiliation of having to attend a meeting like this.

This story is being told "from a child's perspective." By that I mean, from my perspective, because I am the child of an alcoholic; though now an adult, I was raised in the home of an alcoholic. At any age, I will always be the child of an alcoholic, and the words you are reading are my perspective of growing up with an alcoholic father.

My father was born Wilbert Amos Hersom. He somehow was tagged with the nickname "Bub" early in his life. I believe it was one of those names that a friend started calling him on a random basis that just stuck, so his "known" name was Bub Hersom. In fact, many of his friends from later in his life may well not have even known his real name.

First of all, I want to say that my dad was a kind-hearted, do-anything-for-a-friend, kind of guy who never assaulted me or behaved in any type of violent manner like some may have experienced. Nonetheless, his addiction to alcohol eventually cost him his marriage, his relationship with his children, his relationship with his grandchildren, the destruction of his home, the loss of friendships, loss of respect, and ultimately... his life. Basically, everything that at one point in his life meant the world to him, was given up for alcohol. Some may ask or say that if it all meant that much to him, he wouldn't have kept doing it, he would have quit, or it can't be that hard. I'm here to send you the message and to tell you that from my perspective and my experience, alcohol ruined his life on every level and then, ultimately, killed him. Alcohol stole my dad from me and from all of us who loved him at the very young age of only 54!

Is it possible that the alcoholic can't see this...or is it that they see it, but they simply cannot or will not choose to get past it? In the pages coming up, I will show you that he knew exactly what he was giving up and still could not/would not change.

It was February of 1999. I was at home with my wife and four children. The telephone rang. I don't usually answer the phone in the evenings, but for some reason I did this night, instead of my wife or boys answering.

The person on the other end said something like, "Hello, is this the home of Lars Hersom?"

"Yes."

Somehow, some way, I think I knew or felt at that moment that there was something odd about this call, and I was privately, in some small way, praying that it wasn't about my dad. After all, I love this man, it just couldn't be! The person on the other end then introduced himself as a police officer and asked to speak to Lars.

I said, "This is Lars. What is going on?"

He told me, "I'm sorry to be the one to call, but your father passed away and was found at his home."

I dropped to my knees and cried out, "NO.....NO!"

I asked if they knew what had happened, and the officer politely told me that there appeared to not be a struggle of any kind and that Dad had passed away on the couch. This was horrible and—little did I know at the time—only the beginning of the eye-opening experience yet to come.

I was raised in a decent, clean home in a small, rural Iowa community of under 1,000 people. Our home was well-kept, and we were what I would consider a normal mom, dad, and two kids type family. Things that seemed normal to me at the time apparently are not or were not really normal. For example, when I would get home from a basketball, football or baseball game, I never went directly home. I would go to the bar because that is where my dad was. That is where he always was. I would play in pool (billiard) tournaments and cribbage tournaments at the bar, all of which I thought was a normal upbringing.

Some may ask how this has affected my life as far as alcohol goes. I have always taken the position of leading by example for my family and have tried to do the right things in my life as much as I can. With this in mind, I have chosen to not follow the same path as my dad. I am not saying that I never drink. I'm saying that it is rare and it certainly has no control of me or any aspect of my life.

Several years before the event of his death, my mother left him, and for good reason. I never blamed her for leaving. In fact, it makes sense when all is considered. I have to commend her for having the courage to stand up to him and make a decision to move on. I have to believe that she most likely had done all she could to help him and convince him to change. Perhaps the perception I had of our seemingly decent life was covered up...or we, as children, were protected from the reality of these issues by our mother. Looking back, the addiction likely had an effect on my life well before I realized anything was wrong. I'm sure this blindness comes from growing up so close to the issue.

At one point Dad found some woman much younger than him to move in with him, which I never really understood, but I think it was likely due to the hurt that was left behind when he lost his love. This lasted for only a short period of time, and then he was alone again.

I felt sorry for him because I know he still loved my mother but just did not have the ability to make the changes needed to save his marriage and get things back in order. I wanted to help him and had many conversations, seemingly playing the reverse role as the parent trying to keep a child on the right path. From my perspective, I was worried and concerned and tried to help him move in the right direction. In the end, nothing I could say, would make a difference or get through to him. It is quite painful to learn that your words don't get through when you love someone so much and you want to help.

Any time I called to try to see about stopping by the house, it was never a good time for that. Once in a while, he would accommodate my family and me and meet us in a neutral town for dinner, but never anything at the home I grew up in.

After that heartbreaking phone call from the police, I called the funeral home and asked about where my dad's body was. I was again assured that it appeared to be a peaceful passing and that his body was with them. We went over the details as far as facial hair and how to cut his hair, glasses or not, what to wear...what to wear??? My dad had no suit, and I wasn't sure what to do. The funeral parlor representative was a friend of our family and said that he thought he had an old suit we could use if I wanted it, so we did.

Then there were the flower arrangements, where to have the funeral, what about food, who can speak, what church did he go to....did he even go to church anymore and so many more things that I was overwhelmed at some points.

We decided to have his funeral in the funeral home because it would cost less so we purchased the least expensive casket that we could find and went to no expense that we didn't have to do. He had no pre-arranged or pre-paid funeral arrangements or costs, but then again, who would at 54 years old? Since all the costs had to be the burden of the family because Dad had no money whatsoever, we did everything as inexpensively as possible, and it still cost over six thousand dollars. We had financial help from friends and relatives, which was a blessing in its own right.

Did I mention that my dad was 54 years old? That's correct. Let me spell that out for all so it is clear: he was only FIFTY-FOUR YEARS OLD! I am 50 as I sit writing this and simply cannot imagine losing life at such a young age, especially from a self-inflicted disease such as alcoholism.

After the news of my father's death, I immediately called my brother who lived out-of-state to tell him what had happened. He arrived a few days later, to find that nearly all the arrangements were already made. My mother, who had been married to my dad for almost 25 years, was out of town, and we had no way of reaching her. (This was before cell phones were so common.) She was not planning to be back in the area for over a week. By then, the funeral would be over, and Dad would be buried. In hindsight, we all believe that this was the way it was meant to be.

To summarize who my dad was to me, he was bigger than life, as a father typically is—or should be—to his son. I grew up seeing people respect him for who he was and for how he acted. He held a high level of integrity and always did what he said he would do. He was the disciplinarian in our family and was a good steward in the community we lived in. All this was good until the alcohol changed him.

When he started to spend less time with his family and lost his relationship and marriage to the woman he loved, he could not sustain any type of relationship other than that of one with his drinking buddies. He lost his zest for life and ultimately lost his God-given life. What was once so wonderful had been lost due to a relationship with alcohol that became more important than all these beautiful things....so very sad.

CHAPTER 2 - THE HOME

I find myself amazed at how a simple drink can literally destroy a person's life. It is hard to believe that this seemingly innocent beverage can eventually become more important to a person than life, than the love for another person, than any relationship with a son, daughter, wife, mother, father or friend. The power of this drug can be larger than life itself.

Growing up my home was a safe, good, clean and wonderful place to be. I never felt threatened in any way and always felt loved and a part of a family. It was what I would consider a basic middle-class home in a very small community of fewer than a thousand people in northwest Iowa.

We had the typical activities going on, such as barbecues in the summer, playing catch with baseballs and footballs, and so on. My dad taught me how to throw a ball, how to pitch a baseball, how to bat, how to catch, how to tie a knot, make a rope, drive a car, bowl, handle a gun safely, hunt, fish, shoot, worship and to be a person of integrity. He instilled in me many qualities of goodness; it is hard to imagine the changes that were ahead in his life and how these would affect those of us who loved him.

After the call from the police about my dad's death, I received another call about his dog. This dog was quite simply mean. I mean, vicious. No one could go near the dog or my dad if the dog was around. At one point, my dad had a fire in his car, and he had to get a new one. I helped by taking him to a car dealership and picking out something that would work for him. Apparently, after getting the new vehicle and driving it for a period of time (a year or so), the car was repossessed; by then, the dog had destroyed the inside of the vehicle.

When the police called about the dog, they asked me what I wanted to do with it. They told me how it was difficult for them to even get into the house to reach my dad and that they finally got the dog locked up in my dad's car but did not know what to do with him. I asked if they had a place they could take him or if there were any shelters around that would take him because I did not want him anywhere near my home. They said they would take care of it and that was the last I heard of it.

I went to the house the next day to see about cleaning things up and seeing what I had to deal with. I was so completely stunned, disappointed, amazed and shocked at what I saw, that I broke down in tears and shook my head in disbelief. After a quick trip through the house, I headed to the store to get garbage bags and called the city to arrange for a large dumpster to be delivered to the house. It was simply one of the most disgusting and filthy things I have ever seen. I was so surprised at how the home could deteriorate from what I had grown up in to a condition that would be condemned for the toxic waste and filth lying around. It is hard to believe that alcohol could actually take a person from where he was to a place like this and that he had changed his tolerance for this type of behavior to one of acceptance of this low of a quality of life.

There was barely a path through the house with literally piles and piles of garbage sitting around. Empty food containers, open cans of soup partially gone, garbage everywhere...it was truly disgusting. He had put carpet in the kitchen for some odd reason and apparently had experienced a grease fire by the stove which had been put out by a blanket which was still stuck to the carpet and had never been cleaned up. Who knows how long it had been there?

As I picked up the garbage in the living room, I was repeatedly startled by many large mice that had been living in the garbage. I eventually took out over 40 large garbage bags full of trash just to reach a point of being able to walk through the house.

When I reached the kitchen area, I opened the cupboards to start throwing away the old boxes of cake mix and other boxed food items. The top shelf was lined with these types of boxes. I was shocked when I started grabbing boxes to throw away to find that they were all empty! Mice had eaten the backs of the boxes and the contents. Mice had taken over the home that I had grown up in!

Remember the statement about having a dog? Well, he was a large dog similar in size to a German shepherd. The dog had made the second story of the house (where my former bedroom was), the place to go to the bathroom. The entire upstairs of the home was filled with dog feces, and the carpet was obviously soaked with urine. The house smelled so bad that you could hardly breathe. I had to wear a mask to help with the smell and rubber gloves to be sure nothing got on my hands. It was the saddest, most embarrassing and humiliating moment of my life. I am once again left speechless of the deterioration of the quality of life due to the addiction to alcohol.

I had been told by my attorney that I did not have to do anything with the house. I could just go in, get anything I wanted, and walk away.......but I couldn't. For some reason, I felt like I had an obligation to at least clean it up a little so it wasn't so hard to handle what his life had become. I still, to this day, cannot imagine how this could have happened to him. It is simply unbelievable.

The next day, I took my wife and my two oldest children to the house to show them what can happen to a person if they become involved in the use of alcohol or any addictive drug. I spent time with them explaining the details of what had happened and how alcohol had ruined the life of such a wonderful, good person. While these young boys are now grown and are on their own, they still have memories of this issue and understand the negative impact that addiction to any drug can have on a person's life.

During the cleanup of the house, I filled over 40 of the largest leaf-type garbage bags with garbage and filled at least four large metal dumpsters with junk that had accumulated in the house. I spent as much time crying when cleaning up as I did just working. The entire time I was at the house, I was in complete astonishment of the condition everything was in. I still cannot get over how bad it was.

CHAPTER 3 - THE FAMILY

This house had absolutely no resemblance to the home I had grown up in…once a home with loving people and an organized, clean environment. Christmas, Easter, Thanksgiving, Halloween, Fourth of July, Labor Day, Memorial Day and all other holiday celebrations of happiness and joy couldn't possibly have been held in this same home with the same people…..it just is not possible. From my perspective, this represented a disaster that I did not expect.

Our family was a simple, traditional family of a mother, father and two children. We had some other family members who lived in the same small community in the 1960's and early 1970's. They all moved away at various points, and we remained there. In the aftereffects of the addiction to alcohol, my mother has remarried and moved away, and both of us children have moved away as well. When my father passed away, he was the only family member left in the small community; hence, the mention in his (upcoming) notes about being lonely.

We were typical from the standpoint of participating in extra-curricular activities, such as band, baseball, football and basketball.

My parents attended many, if not all of the games and always supported us in the things we wanted to participate in.

After a game, it was typical to go to the bar to see Dad before going home. Whether an away game or a home game, whether it was 9 p.m. or 11 p.m., when the game was over, when the bus returned to town, I could almost always find him there. Amazingly, even though I spent a good portion of my life at the bar, I have never been a "drinker." Whether consciously or sub-consciously, I just never developed a desire for drinking or for being inebriated. I'm not saying that I have never taken a drink of alcohol, but I am saying that I have no interest in making it a habit.

My parents would go out on Saturday nights to the bars to go dancing to whatever band was in town. It was not unusual for them to come back to our home, bringing several friends to continue to party until the wee hours of the morning. My brother and I would be asleep well before they came home, but we would typically wake up and listen or try to look downstairs through the floor registers to see what was going on. Usually, it was a continuation of the party, including plenty of drinking and a breakfast of some kind.

On a more positive note, my dad did, indeed, teach us to handle weapons safely, to shoot, hunt, fish and play ball, and he was there for us...until alcohol took over his life completely. I had always looked forward to the day that Dad would be able to share some of these same attributes with his grandchildren. This is one of the many things that is so sad about the loss. The awesome, wonderful things that will never be, all because of the addiction to booze.

The largest impact to Dad's dedication and commitment to the family was, without question, the divorce with my mother. Prior to the divorce, he had made life miserable for my mother.

I have no doubt that she did all she could to bring him to a place for them to have a chance at saving their marriage.

He, however, had taken refuge with alcohol and was convinced that it was everyone else who had a problem, but he was fine. You can see evidence of this in his notes at the end of the book.

I had attempted to get close to him and to find out all that was going on in his life at different points, with no success. Looking back at the conversations, it is clearer now than then, that he was being evasive and not really answering my questions.

He knew he had a serious problem and was so engulfed in the web of deceit that he was constantly aware of what he was doing by always protecting his relationship and addiction to alcohol. I feel so sorry for him every time I think of how terrible it had to have been for him, even though he may not have truly been consciously aware. I personally believe that the alcohol had to numb his consciousness to a point of not being aware of the actual impact it was having on his life.

I remember going hunting with my Dad; in reality, for him it was really a time to get away and drink while I hunted. Looking back, I would be dropped off at a place out in the country, given some directions of where to walk and would be picked up at the end of the hunt. Sometimes it was a short walk of a mile or less and sometimes a walk of several hours. Most times, there was alcohol in the car. In fact, I remember a time when I was helping my grandmother dig potatoes from their large garden, and while I was driving her over to the garden, the glove box came open in the car and a bottle of alcohol came rolling out.

I remember saying, "That's my dad's."

Grandma already knew and put it away without even a blink or really saying anything that I can recall.

While I continue to have a close relationship with my mother, the family has been ultimately torn apart by the addiction. First, the addictive behavior started as seemingly innocent drinking at the bar with friends. This was followed over time by us children growing up and moving out of the home. I believe that the impact of the house being empty and a weakened relationship between my mother and father made the attraction to alcohol even stronger.

This was followed by the divorce which, from my perspective, pushed the addiction to new levels. At some point around the time we kids moved out of the home, Dad was diagnosed with adult onset diabetes, which, of course, is a prescription for disaster when combined with alcoholism.

I'm sure he was embarrassed and depressed when the divorce happened and that this event represented the point of no return. He became withdrawn from the family and would avoid any contact with any of us.

CHAPTER 4 - THE HOSPITAL

Twice during the last couple years of his life, my mother called to let me know that my dad was in the hospital. She had divorced him and was living in a house basically right in his back yard. She would check on him from time to time. Twice when she checked on him, she found him in a comatose state lying half on the bed and half off, foaming at the mouth.

Mom called 911 for an ambulance. They came, revived him, and got him to the hospital. I visited him in the hospital and tried to help him understand how serious it was.

I would tell him, "Dad, we love you and want you in our lives!"

When he was ready to be released from the hospital, he would call my mom to come and get him. She would in turn, call me, and I would leave my job to go pick him up at the hospital and take him home.

I would always take him somewhere to eat and use the time to try to reach him and help him understand that I was there to help and did not want to lose him. This was a total reversal of roles for us. When I was younger, he was the one who would preach to me and help give me advice about what I needed to do to become a good person and stay on the right track; now I was taking the role of the adult, preaching about the dangers of what he was experimenting with and the things he stood to lose if he did not change his ways. I tried desperately to help him understand how much he was loved and needed in our lives. I had four children at home and they all needed to experience a relationship with their grandpa.

I know he told my mom that he really didn't want me to pick him up at the hospital because of "the talk" he knew I would have with him...so sad that it had come to this.

When I would ask him if he understood what he was missing out on (after I had spent hours talking to him about the details), he would say that he understood, but mostly by just nodding his head. I had a very difficult time getting him to engage in any conversation of any depth whatsoever. I kept telling him that I loved him and wanted him to be part of my life, our family's life, his grandchildren's lives. We all wanted him to be a part of our lives, and I made sure he knew it.

Even with explaining this in a face-to-face conversation, I could not get through to him. The depth of the relationship—the grip that alcohol had on him—was much stronger than that of his wife, his sons, his grandchildren, and his extended family. He had positive motivation from all of us to change. He had negative motivation from law enforcement in the form of losing his license to drive, paying large fines, and being put in jail.

I can only thank God that he never was in a car accident that injured someone else. What a tragedy that would have been.

CHAPTER 5 - THE FUNERAL

The funeral was one of the most difficult things for me to deal with of anything in my life to date. We had the arrangements made to handle everything at the funeral home with the exception of a small coffee reception at the church that we attended when I was growing up.

Before the funeral could start, arrangements for so many things had to be done, so many decisions to be made. What should Dad wear? What should we do about flowers? Should we have a guest book? How should his hair be cut? Moustache or not? Open or closed casket? Which casket, a vault, and headstone? What should it say? How were we going to pay for everything? Whom should we notify? Who should carry Dad's casket?

Among the most difficult, which was a surprise to me, was choosing the people to carry the casket. There were a few volunteers in the people my dad now called friends. These people were some of those that he never would have probably even been associated with as I was growing up, but now, they were the crowd that he called his friends. There were still a couple spots to fill, but no one wanted to do it.

All I could think as we were dealing with this was that he had apparently alienated the large group of friends he had accumulated through the years. My dad was one of these guys who knew just about everyone and would do anything for any of his friends. He would help them in a time of need and be there whenever there was something that had to be done with no repayment expected, other than a thank you and usually a cold beer or two. In short, Dad had been just a really good guy that people knew they could count on, and he was a generally happy person.

Not being able to reach my mother was a big issue for me and for my brother. What should we do? Have the funeral? Bury him? Wait? We made the decision to go forward with things since they were no longer married and hoped she would understand. In the end, she not only understood what we did, but was sorry for us to have to deal with all this on our own without her help. I think the good Lord wanted it this way to make it easier for her to accept. We had done it all, including burying him, before she even knew it happened. Good or bad, some might disagree, but for our family and the circumstances we had to deal with, this worked best for us.

My wife suggested that we make a photo mural of him to have in the entrance of the funeral home for people to see and wanted to focus on the good times and earlier years to help people remember who he was and not who or what he had become. It was a great idea, and I loved having it there. I remember crying when I saw it, and it still brings tears to my eyes when I think of how it was done. No question, I loved this man very much and, for quite some time, tried to figure out what, if anything, I could have done differently to change this dreadful outcome.

My wife and children, brother and a few relatives were there to greet people when they came in to the funeral home. The main relatives (outside of my family and my brother) were my dad's sister and her husband who helped however they could. His side of the family was quite small. He had two sisters, of which only one was able to make it to the funeral.

I saw many old friends at the funeral home, which was the highlight of the event, if there could be one. Once everyone had been greeted and seated, it was time for the farewell. My brother and I had met with the pastor and had chosen a few passages and highlights of his life to be read.

As I took my seat in the funeral home, I looked around. Every room in every direction was filled with people! Holy cow! I couldn't believe it! Even though it had been difficult finding people to commit to carrying his casket, there was an outpour of people representing those whose lives he had touched and those who had touched his. I was shocked, happy, sad, full of tears and appreciation, all at the same moment.

Earlier that morning before we left our home to travel to the funeral 20 miles away, I went to my basement to collect my thoughts on a pad of paper of some things that I wanted to say to whoever would show up. The note I wrote to say that day went like this:

"I want to thank you all for coming for my dad's funeral. I want you to all know that the reason my mother is not here, is because she is out of town and has not been able to be reached. We know she would have wanted to be here, but due to the circumstances, it was not possible."

"Most of you in this room knew my dad before he became the person he had. I ask that you each remember him for who he once was, as a kind, giving person who would do anything for a friend and not for what had become of his life."

"My dad had given me a plaque years ago that I have hanging by the tool bench in my shop." On this plaque was a description of what my father's name meant to him and what it should mean to me. It describes how his name was clean when he received it from his father and how it was the same when I received it from him. There is mention of things that are lost and things that come and go but describes how your name is there for your entire life and is your personal responsibility to maintain the integrity of your name. I found this to be very important given that his name was intact when I received it and I have done my best to keep it that way throughout my life. Even though he had fallen to this dreadful disease, he was still a person of honor and integrity. This poem, "Your Name", by Edgar Albert Guest, has been an inspiration to me to do my best to preserve our family name and integrity. I believe that God brought the thought to me to use this poem during my father's funeral, to help bring peace to me and to let the group know how I felt.

During the reading of the writing on the plaque, I broke down, and I sensed that there was a funeral home full of people following my lead. I could not get myself back together and on track until after it was read. While I knew it was not possible for him to be brought back to us, I just wanted him to come back and give it another try! Anything, just come back!

We all went to the car to prepare for the trip to the cemetery. As I was sitting in my car, one of my dad's old friends came out of the funeral home.

As he was walking past my car, he said, "Don't worry, Lars, we will all remember him as he was, and he was a great guy and, by the way, he would have been so proud of you for the words you spoke."

I thanked him for the comment and broke down again.

At the cemetery were, what I would consider, a rather large group of people. I can't even remember what was said by the Pastor, but I do recall that it was very cold outside.

After everyone had left, the funeral parlor representative, my brother, and I were alone by the side of the casket. I don't recall seeing my little brother cry much, if at all, prior to that moment. He reached out, put his hand on the casket, and started to weep loudly. I put my arm around him to comfort him; at that point, I had no more tears to shed, at least for the moment.

We spent a short amount of time by the casket and said our last goodbyes. Following the service at the cemetery was a reception back at the church. I heard many nice comments about my brother, my family, and me. People commented how things had gone so well, and how nice it was to see us again. It was all the typical pleasantries that are said at things like this. While I was appreciative of all this, the fact was that my father was gone, and I was having a very difficult time dealing with the loss.

CHAPTER 6 - THE NOTES

As I was cleaning out the massive amount of garbage and debris in the house, I found a set of hand written notes that were written by my father. These notes appeared to be structured in a way that I believed them to be part of the classes he had to attend for alcoholism. I included the actual notes for you to see that he indeed did know exactly what he was missing out on and that he recognized that something had a hold on him from which he could not free himself. I think he reached a point where he felt there was no return and did not have the strength, desire, or will to fight this horrible disease.

My wife and I immediately realized that these notes should be kept…that they could someday provide inspiration in some way. We had no idea at the time how or when or what the format would be for Dad's notes to help people. Perhaps sharing them with others will align their past purpose with other people's present lives and may influence their futures. Somehow this message may touch the heart of someone and help to improve his or her quality of life. Perhaps it could even save someone from the suffering of the loss of a loved one at such a young age.

These notes have proven to be a great resource for me to find some kind of peace in understanding what Dad was going through and how difficult it truly was for him on a daily basis. His letter to alcohol and comments about how his addiction had disrupted his life were some of the most important things that gave me some insight in to what he was facing.

Although I truly cannot and will not ever understand what it is like to be an alcoholic and how challenging it is to overcome this disease, I can truly tell you how it feels to be on the other end of the relationship. Because the addiction takes control of the person, at some point the alcohol becomes more important than any relationship, any person, any true love, any feeling other than that of being with their new friend named Alcohol. It makes it impossible to maintain a relationship with the person you love and are willing to do anything for. From my perspective, the alcohol changes the person in ways that keep others from being allowed to help and from maintaining a connection which is so important in any relationship of love and respect.

It seems like the alcohol becomes a body guard that tries to become your best friend, and when you allow this to happen, you lose all sense of reality for those who truly love you. The "body guard" then seems to be able to convince the person that it is more important than anything else in life and to become insensitive to what other people say and do to try to help. The "body guard" has such a strong will, that others can rarely, if ever, get past the guard and touch the heart of the person who is guarded. This may seem strange or a stretch to some for an analogy, but it is the way I felt when trying to get through to my father.

If there is one thing that any person takes from this book, I hope and pray it is that of hope and a realization that those in your life want to help and desire to have you in their lives. No one wants to see someone suffer from any disease, but please understand that when you are an alcoholic, you will be heavily influenced by your new friend in a web of deceit, lies, and grief that will destroy your home, your relationships, your attitude towards those you love and eventually will take your life if you continue to drink.

It just simply does not have to be that way. Trust others to help. Believe the ones who love you when they try to convince you to seek help and accept their help. Perhaps one of the hardest things to do or accept is that your circle of friends and the places you go need to change for you to get your life back. It will likely be better than it ever has been if you trust those who love and support you.

Next are copies of the notes handwritten by my father:

UNMANAGEABLES

My wife Leaving me.
My youngest son moving to California.
My mother moving away from me.
my frindes drinking when I can't.
my father dying.
my getting 2 owI's.
my having diabetis Witch makes me disabled
my not being able to play golf anymore
my not being able to drive.
my having to attend A.A.
my having two sisters Witch are Very happy
my having to spend time in jail.
my having to pay fines.
my having to eat my own cooking
My having to do thngs other people want
    Instead of what I want
my oldest son having a very good job.
my oldest son having a very happy family
my youngest son doing very well in
    Hollywood California
my not being able to do things I want
    Without help from others.
my having money problems becose of
    my liminited income.
my X wife remaring Twice after
    we were devoriced.

25

My Sons feelings about there mothers
Last Two marriges.
My grandchirdlens relationship with
their grandmother after our divorce.
My friend's feelings of frindship or
oblications Toward me.

Insanities

My using alcohol.

My thinking I could quit any time without help.

my thinking alcohol would not change my way of Life.

my thinking I could do Things as well drinking as I could Sober.

my Trying to make people think I was Sober when I was not.

my Trying to Fool the police into thinking I was Sober.

my mixing the use of alcohol with the use of deadly wepons.

my thinking alcohol would help keep me warm when I was Snomobiling

my using alcohol to help me Find the courage I needed.

my trying to make my friends think I could drink more than they could

my drinking while in treetment

my thinking I could Think stright while under the Influnce of alcohol

my thinking Alcohol would not affect the way I played sports

my telling myself that alcohol would not affect my health

my Thinking alcohol will help me
   overcome my problems.
my thinking I could hide me exsesive
   drinking from my family
my feeling that drinking makes me
   a more likebale person.
my beliveling I can change from an
   alcohodic to normal drinker.
my beliving that alcohol has to be
   Included in everything I do.
my thinking I have to use alcohol
   to make friends.
my Thinking I don't have to change
   Play pens and playmates
my thinking my drinking would
   not affect my children
my thinking that drinking would
   Improve my Social stauts.
my driving while I was under
   the Inflance of alcohol
my thinking people would respect
   Me as much drunk as sober
my feeling people would not know I
   was drinking alown
my Thinking I could quit forever
   by quiting a few days

my beliving that alcohol is not
adictable to me.

My thinking alcohol would not
affect my reflexes

my thinking that alcohol was not
having an effect on my home life

my beliving you had to be drinking
to have a good time

my thinking my drinking was not
affecting my ~~manage~~ manage

my letting alcohol play such a
big part in my life

My spending money on alcohol that could
have been spent on better things

my letting alcohol affect my work
Without drinking on the job

my not attmiting that alcohol was
taking over my life.

My making sure I had access to a
drink at all times.

my thinking there was a diference
between beer + hard liquor

my letting alcohol come between
me and my higher power

My letting alcohol have enough power
me to put me in Jail

my Letting alcohol come before
Spending time with my grandchildren
my Letting alcohol pick out the
people I hang around with
my Letting alcohol come between
me and my sisters & my mother

Sucesses

Graduating from high scool
Being captian of the basketball
   team my senior year
Lettering in basketball,
   baseball & track
Rasing two boys to become
   Sucesseful adults
Being able to suport my wife
   and family for 25 years.
Coaching Little League, babe routh
   and townteam base ball teams
Helping my kids out when they
   needed me
Helping my dad and mom run a
   Sucessful busness when I was
   In high school
Doing all the ~~feeling~~ remodiling and repairs
   around The house myself
Bringing my children up in a
   Christchen home
Teaching my boys how to fish &
   hunt when they were young.
Connoing and camping with my
   family.
Bringing up my boys as boy Scouts

31

faliers

Starting to smoke when I
   was young
Not being home all the times
   when I should have.
Lying to my wife about where I
   spent some of my late nites
   when I was not at home.
Breaking the law by stealing when
   I was young from my foaks.
trying to hide my drinking from
   my family
Drinking to much when I should be
   takaing care of my family
Drinking and driving and spending
   time in Jail.
Not learning the first time I got
   picked up for OWI.
Not spending enough time with my
   grandkids becouse of my drinking.
Letting my drinking interfier with
   my church going.

things that don't
~~enclose~~ alachol
enclude

going tochurch
playin baseball with my
Grandkids.
going fishing with my
grankids
doing wood working
walking my dog
camping with my grandkids
Picknicking with my
Grandkids

1   Becose I am a christen
2   Becose I am concidered one of
    the better pool players In town.
3   Becose I raise a garden for
    me and my neabors.
4   Becouse I was a scout leader
    when my kids were scouts
5   Becose I am trustworthy
6. Becose people like me
7   Becose I am honost
8   Becose I treet others kindly
9   Becose I am a good cook
10 Becose I was good in ataletics
11 Becose I was good on two
    musical Instermints.
12 Becose I raised my family for
    25 years
13 Becose I am a woodworker
14 Becore I try to help people
    when I can
15 Becose I keep intotch with
    my mother on a weekly basis
16 Becose I helped raise two good
    boys
17 Becose I helped my foaks and
    did not fight with them

18 Becouse I do not blame anyone
for any of my wrong doings

19 Becose I helped to coach
some baseball teams

20 Becose my boys were not afarde
to come to me with there problems

21 Becose I work hard at the things
I want

22 Becose I care about my kids and
grand kids

23 Becose I was a good booler
In the past years.

24 Becose I am In this treetement
Program.

25 Becose I have quit drinking hopefuly
For the last Time

This is my letter
    to Alochol
I guess I won't need to find
an address becose you seem to
be everwhere I look

Well I met you about 30 some
odd years ago. I rember it
well. A frind of mine brought
you home from service and
interduced you to some of us
younger guys.
The first few years we semed
to get along like good friends.
we spent more and more time
togeather as time went along.
all the time you trying make
me think we were just good
friends butt all the time you
were setting me up for the big
fall
Now you have interduced me
to some people. you introduced
me to some police officers I
dident realy care to know.
now after 30 some years of
knowing one another you have aged
me about 50 years and you seem

to Appear the same way you
always looked.
I have said good by to you once
or twice during the years but we
always seemed to get togeather
again but this time I ~~feel~~ feel
I have more help ~~on~~ on my side
so I hope this is the last good
by I have to say

I hope I don't see
you later

Wilber

CHAPTER 7 - THE END (...OR IS IT?)

After the funeral was over when I was dealing with the closure of some of the debt left behind, I realized that Dad may have thought the end was near. One of his friends stopped to see me on one of the days that I was cleaning Dad's house. He brought a rifle that my dad had in his gun collection.

When he handed me the rifle, he said, "Your dad wanted me to give this to you. He had the scope mounted and had it sighted in for you."

It was one sign that Dad knew the end was near as this was something he had always wanted to do for me.

I took care of some of Dad's small, local bills that he owed people for things like lawn mowing, which really wasn't much at all. My attorney again had advised me that I did not have to do anything at all because it was not my responsibility, but I could do anything I felt I wanted to with no obligation.

At one point I received a call from a loan company that had performed a walk by assessment of the home property and loaned him some money based on the walk-around appraisal. It was apparent that he had taken the money from the loan to pay off some debts he had with people in the community because it was relatively recent, and he had no money left to his name anywhere. He had no life insurance either.

The home loan company tried to place guilt on me to convince me it was my responsibility as his son to pay this debt. I had already met with my attorney and knew that I had absolutely no obligation to this lending institution whatsoever. At one point, I did have thoughts of cleaning out the house and selling it to cover the funeral costs, but as soon as I found out that it was fully mortgaged, the idea was off.

Then I started getting calls from the county assessor's office at the county court house asking me to pay the back taxes on his property. Again, I had checked with my attorney and was advised that I had absolutely no obligation to any of this debt. Since the house was fully mortgaged and the property had no value, I made no attempt to pay the taxes. I told the people who were calling that I would not be paying the taxes and that the home would eventually be in the hands of the lenders. The reason they even knew who to call was because this is a small community and a small county so everyone pretty much knows everyone. The people at the courthouse knew that I was his son, so they called me.

What an uncomfortable position to be put in! I know my father did not put me in that position on purpose. In fact, I'm sure he never gave a thought to how or what the issues would be that were left for his family to have to deal with. I was never angry with him for leaving a mess to deal with, but it would have been nice to not have to even think of the things that were left behind.

I took some of the memorable things from the home, placed all the clothes, food, garbage and junk in the dumpsters, picked up things a bit, took one last walk through and closed the back door for the last time. I felt my heart sink as I walked to my car to leave for the last time. I cried because I didn't want to believe what had happened over these last few days. I felt so ashamed, so disappointed, so upset, so sad for all this, yet I felt more strongly than ever that I needed to be sure my family was led by example to do the right things in life. I hope my father can look down on me as his son and us as his family and smile with pride and love and know that in the end, something good has come from his life.

Although the end was so painful as in any loss of a parent, especially at a young age of only 54, I hope that sharing this story will inspire someone to find the strength to fight alcoholism and believe in someone who loves them. It is my hope that someone will find peace, joy and an inner strength needed to recover and rejoin the lives of those who love them so they can recognize all the love and need for them in life.

I lost my dad at a very young age to a stranger that led him away with deceit and lies. I hope and pray that someone can learn and believe that any life is worth fighting for, that any person may change if they personally desire to change, and the support and assistance of others can help them find success in recovery.

If you are struggling with an addiction to alcohol and you have turned away from your family or loved ones, please, I implore you to turn to them, call on them, ask them to support you and encourage you through the recovery. You will likely find a level of love, understanding, comfort, joy and support that are so worth the effort and pain you may need to go through to find your way back.

Although I feel pain and I miss my dad, I take peace in knowing that he was a good person and that he is in a place with no addiction, no deceit, no lies and no pain. Now Dad is in a place of love, joy, and freedom and knows that we loved him so much, and we are happy he is struggling no more.

From the perspective of the person afflicted with the challenges of this disease, I hope you can somehow find a way to believe that your life will be better when you choose to change and that you can be humble enough to recognize that there is a problem and ask for help.

From the perspective of the child, spouse, parent, relative or friend who knows someone afflicted with this disease, I encourage you to fight for your loved ones and to let them know you are there for them. It may be discouraging because of their commitment to alcohol that seems to outweigh their relationship with anyone else; however, they are worth any effort you can put in to trying to make them aware of what they are missing in life.

From either perspective I want to encourage you to step up and take responsibility for your actions, for your relationships with your loved ones. The slimy liquid of deceit is full of evil intentions and will do its best to cloud your views and take you away from all the things that matter most in life.

I am certainly not proclaiming to know it all or to have a certificate in any type of formal training that would make my opinions official advice in some capacity; nonetheless, I can offer my insight from the perspective of a person who grew up in the home of an alcoholic. I am someone who has lived this first-hand and lost a father at an early age. I'm sure most would agree that there is an unwritten certificate of knowledge and competence that comes with such experience.

If you are struggling with this disease, please consider changing your circle of friends, changing the places you frequent, changing your outlook on alcohol....CHANGING YOUR LIFE....in the most wonderful way imaginable....

This is not the end...it is YOUR beginning...the beginning for someone you love. Don't lose your loved one, and don't lose your life.

From my perspective, you are worth the effort it takes to change your life in a positive way!

From my perspective, you are in a position to make a positive difference in the life of someone who needs your help and support!

From my perspective...I choose life, love, peace, and happiness over all else. Please consider giving it your best effort and leave no cards on the table, no regrets of things you wish you would have done or said, no worries or thoughts of "what if." Know you have done all you can do!

May the strength of God's will be with all who are pursuing an improved quality of life and may His wisdom guide you through the challenges in your life.

Again...

Dedication

Respectfully written in loving memory of my father,
Wilbert "Bub" Amos Hersom
I love you, Dad. I always have and always will.

ABOUT THE AUTHOR

My father lost his life due to an addiction to alcohol. I have been searching for a way to reach out to the world to communicate and share my experience of growing up in the home of an alcoholic. My hope is to attempt to help people to understand that this drug becomes more important than anything else in their lives. I hope to encourage each person to not give up, to believe that under the appearance of carelessness for themselves and others, there is a person who, at the root of the issue, really does understand what is going on, but cannot or will not take what they consider a risk of leaving this powerful friend behind and come back to the ones that love them. With all this in mind, this book is written from the perspective of a person who has grown up in the home of an alcoholic. So....from my perspective....I will always be the son or the child of an alcoholic. My perspective is reality.

I have grown up and live in a small midwest community of less than 1,500 people. I am the Branch Manager at the company I work for and share my life with my beautiful wife and four wonderful boys. I believe in leading by example in my life in order to pass along a commitment to God, a trustworthy attitude and a life with deep passion, gratitude, peace, love and joy. I sincerely hope that I can touch the lives of others and change the path of people in a manner that brings these attributes to them.

Printed in the United States
By Bookmasters